RETIREMENT PLANNING GUIDE 2023

How to navigate major financial decisions to make your retirement years the best of your life

BY

Tom Miller

© Copyright 2023 - All rights reserved.

It is not legal to reproduce, duplicate, or transmit any part of this document in either electronic means or printed format. Recording of this publication is strictly prohibited and any storage of this document is not allowed unless with written permission from the publisher except for the use of brief quotations in a book review.

Table of Contents

INTRODUCTION 6

CHAPTER 1. EARLY RETIREMENT 8

    START SAVING AND INVESTING EARLY 9

    INCREASE YOUR SAVINGS RATE GRADUALLY 10

    CONSIDER WORKING A SIDE HUSTLE OR STARTING A SMALL BUSINESS 11

    PAY OFF HIGH-INTEREST DEBT 13

    MAKE A PLAN AND STICK TO IT 14

CHAPTER 2. RETIREMENT PITFALLS 15

    RETIRING WITHOUT SETTING ASIDE THE FIRST THREE YEARS OF INCOME 15

    BORROWING FROM YOUR RETIREMENT FUND 16

    FORGETTING TO ACCOUNT FOR HEALTH CARE COSTS 17

CHAPTER 3. PLANNING FOR HEALTH CARE EXPENSES 20

    MEDICARE SUPPLEMENTAL INSURANCE 21

    DISABILITY INSURANCE 21

    HEALTH SAVINGS ACCOUNTS (HSAS) AND ROTH IRAS FOR HEALTH SAVINGS 23

    HEALTH CARE OPTIONS BEFORE AGE 65 23

CHAPTER 4. WHAT TO DO IF YOU DON'T HAVE ENOUGH SAVINGS 25

    WORKING LONGER TO BOOST SAVINGS 26

GENERATING INCOME IN RETIREMENT 27

CREATING A RETIREMENT PLAN 29

CHAPTER 5. HOUSING DECISIONS 31

DO RETIREES MOVE? 32

CHARACTERISTICS OF A GOOD PLACE TO LIVE IN RETIREMENT 34

REVERSE MORTGAGES ARE NOT FOR ELDERLY HOMEOWNERS 36

DECIDING TO STAY AT HOME OR DOWNSIZE 37

RENTING VS. BUYING A HOME 38

CHAPTER 6. PHYSICAL AND MENTAL HEALTH IN RETIREMENT 41

HOW THE BODY CHANGES AFTER AGE 65 43

HOW TO STAY ACTIVE AND ENGAGED AS YOU GET OLDER 44

CHAPTER 7. NON-FINANCIAL ASPECTS OF RETIREMENT 46

APPROACHING RETIREMENT AS A SINGLE PERSON OR WITH A PARTNER? 47

FINDING YOUR PURPOSE AND PASSIONS 48

SOCIAL INTERACTIONS IN RETIREMENT 50

CREATING A DAILY ROUTINE AND MAINTAINING RELATIONSHIPS 51

CHAPTER 8. MEDICARE AND HEALTH INSURANCE 53

HEALTH INSURANCE OPTIONS BEFORE MEDICARE ELIGIBILITY 54

UNDERSTANDING MEDICARE'S ABCDS 56

 USING MEDICARE'S RESEARCH PROGRAM 58

 ANNUAL OPEN ENROLLMENT OPTIONS AND BUDGETING FOR HEALTH CARE EXPENSES 60

CHAPTER 9. HOW RETIREMENT HAS CHANGED AND MAY CHANGE IN THE FUTURE 63

 FUTURE TRENDS AND POTENTIAL CHANGES IN RETIREMENT PLANNING 65

CHAPTER 10. SAVING AND BUDGETING FOR THE COMING YEARS 68

 MAXIMIZING EMPLOYER 401(K) CONTRIBUTIONS 69

 REDUCING EXPENSES IS A GOOD IDEA 70

 BUDGETING BEFORE RETIREMENT 72

CONCLUSION 74

Introduction

Retirement planning is the process of determining how to financially support yourself during retirement, when you are no longer earning a regular income from employment.

One retirement statistic that should be on your radar is that the average age for someone to receive their Social Security benefits is increasing, and the probability of means testing will be higher as people live longer. According to a recent Harris Poll survey, nearly three-quarters of the adults surveyed within ten years of retiring said that they planned to achieve their dreams while in a less-pressurized stage of their lives. This includes the likes of launching a side hustle or even entering the workforce.

A recent Investopedia study found that the majority of Gen Xers were confident in their financial acumen. More than half of them are using retirement products to increase their wealth while minimizing their tax liability.

Aside from the typical bucket of cash, consider other options such as part-time work, second careers, and even a cruise to the Caribbean. If you are lucky, you may be able to achieve your dreams while still living a relatively modest lifestyle.

It is true that the best way to save for a retirement is to avoid all risk, but there are some creative solutions to this challenge. One strategy is geographic arbitrage, which can lower the overall cost of living. Another involves a phased retirement, which can allow you to afford to enjoy a golden retirement without putting a dent in your savings.

Finally, you may want to consider a hybrid approach to save for retirement, such as a combination of a 401(k) and a IRA. Although the golden years are still a long way off, you can prepare for them by setting up a retirement budget, and learning about financial products that can help you meet your lifestyle goals.

Chapter 1.
Early Retirement

If you are thinking of retiring early, you may be wondering what steps you need to take to accomplish your goal. Retiring early can offer you many benefits, including more time with family and friends, healthier living, and the ability to pursue new interests and hobbies. However, retiring early also requires careful planning and financial discipline. Keeping in mind the following tips can help you achieve your goals.

- One of the first things you will need to do when planning to retire early is to determine your desired lifestyle and location.
- You should then create a budget to plan your expenses and to establish a monthly savings goal. When you know how much money you need to spend,

you can set up automatic transfers to your retirement accounts. It's important to keep in mind that you will need to cut costs to ensure that you can reach your savings goals. This will decrease your housing expenses and commuting costs.

Once you have your budget and monthly and annual savings goals, it's time to start thinking about investments. Before you make a final decision, it's a good idea to check out an early retirement calculator to determine how much you'll need.

In addition, you should be sure to budget your funds wisely. Eating out can add up, so you may want to start cutting back on those too.

- Another option is to consider retiring in a more affordable location. If you live in a large city, you might want to consider moving to a smaller town. Early retirement is not for everyone, however. Those who are in poor health, for instance, may not be able to take advantage of the benefits that an early retirement offers. Also, there are those who would prefer to work longer before retiring. While it may be tempting to leave the workforce earlier, you will need to think long and hard about whether this is the best option for you. Unless you're in a highly lucrative field, you may not be able to make this work for you.

Start saving and investing early

A great way to make your money go farther is to learn how to invest. Compounding interest is a great way to boost your savings, especially if you're just starting out. Additionally, you can use your employer's matching program to help boost your nest egg. Some employers even raise the rate you save to as much as three percent of your income.

Investing in a 401(k) or similar plan will allow you to stash away funds at your place of employment, where the company will automatically deposit it into your account. Many companies will even match up to six percent of your salary, which can make it easier to reach your financial goals.

Investing is one of the most challenging aspects of preparing for your golden years, but it's a smart move for any retiree. In fact, a recent survey from TD Ameritrade showed that 75% of adults ages 70 and older would actually encourage their younger selves to do something similar. Investing earlier can give you a leg up on the competition, especially when it comes to building your retirement nest egg.

Starting to save early also makes it easier to take advantage of compounding. The premise behind compounding is simple. Rather than simply putting your money into a bank account and waiting for the bank to pay you back, you invest it and let it grow over time. What's more, the accumulated interest earned on your investments can actually increase the value of your portfolio.

Despite all the benefits of saving and investing, it's important to realize that there are risks involved. This is why it's best to invest in investments that offer dividends, and reinvest them if possible. Although it's hard to predict the future, it's still a good idea to keep a close eye on your portfolio to track its performance.

Increase your savings rate gradually

A good starting point for increasing your savings rate is to create a savings plan. By establishing a regular savings routine, you will be able to avoid the temptation to make unnecessary purchases and you may find yourself with extra cash on hand.

To increase your savings rate, you can start by setting a reasonable amount of money to save each month. Although the average American spends $18,500 per year on food, clothes, and other necessities, you can easily set aside at least a couple of thousand dollars each month. Similarly, you can make an effort to avoid getting more credit cards. The more you save, the more you can afford to purchase the items you want, when you want them.

Creating a savings plan is a good idea, but it is not always possible to save at 100% of your salary. It is also a good idea to put some of your earnings in tax-advantaged investment accounts, such as a 401(k) or a Roth IRA. One of the easiest ways to save for retirement is to start an automatic investment program that will help you grow your money.

If you already have an emergency fund in place, you can supplement it by adding 1% to it each month. Saving for retirement should also be a priority, but you don't have to sacrifice your other life priorities just to reach this goal.

For starters, you can open a tax-advantaged savings account with a bank, such as Ally Bank. Ideally, you should start with the minimum required contribution and increase it a few percentage points each month, to ensure your savings keep building.

Using a budget to save for your retirement is the best way to ensure you can achieve your lifelong financial goals. Increasing your savings rate gradually, the smart way, will ensure your finances are in tip top shape when you retire.

Consider working a side hustle or starting a small business

Starting a side hustle can give you the flexibility to pursue your passions and increase your savings at the same time. You can find out what type of business you want to get started by conducting a little research. Your local SCORE office can also help you figure out what type of side gig is right for you. While working a side hustle is a great way to put your skills to work, it is not an easy endeavor. Unless you are willing to devote your entire life to your side gig, it may be difficult to achieve your dream of owning your own business.

In the early days of your side gig, you may not have a lot of money to invest in it. You may need to find a small loan or sign up for a loan with your bank. Alternatively, you might be able to find some of the funding you need via unconventional sources such as crowdfunding.

If you are lucky enough to have the funds to spare, you might want to hire a virtual assistant to do some of the legwork for you. However, you should be aware that it can be expensive to find a quality virtual assistant, so you might be better off looking at hiring an employee with more experience.

For your side gig to be a success, it will need to have a business credit profile. This will require you to open a small business bank account and make sure that your financials are in order.

A well-written business plan will also help you achieve your goals. An effective plan will contain an executive summary, an operations plan, marketing strategy, and a financial plan. These will help you keep track of expenses and ensure that your side venture is a success.

Getting the name and logo of your side hustle right is important. When choosing your business name, you should consider the size of the customer base you wish to serve and choose a name that isn't too similar to your own. Also, be careful about the spelling of your name. Some states have specific licenses for starting a side business.

Taking the time to write out a business plan will help you decide if your idea is a good one. The right business plan will help you grow your side gig and keep you afloat when the economy takes a nosedive.

Pay off high-interest debt

One of the best options is to use a debt consolidation loan. You can also get the best rate for your needs by pre-qualifying before you make your decision. Your monthly payment may be fixed for several years, and you can have more control over your financial future. Even better, you can avoid having to manage multiple credit cards.

The credit card company can lower your rates if you show them that you are a good payment customer. For example, if you have a balance transfer credit card, you can lower your monthly payments to zero for almost two years.

Another option is to cut your expenses in a few areas, such as entertainment and health. You can also find out if your employer offers flexible hours, or if you can work part-time to save money.

Finally, you can try to find a way to increase your income. If you have the means, taking on a second job, selling unused items, or picking up extra tasks around the house may be a good way to boost your income. In addition, if you have the time, consider starting a savings account.

There are also various debt management programs out there. The best way to pay off your high-interest debt is to make the right decisions. This includes choosing the right types of loans, making sure to stick with a repayment plan, and looking for the most favorable interest rates. This can help prevent you from making poor spending decisions, and introducing new habits that lead to more debt in the future.

Make a plan and stick to it

The first thing to do when attempting to plan is to define your goal. When you know how long it will take, you can set a realistic time frame and be prepared to meet the challenge. For example, if you are trying to lose weight, you might consider writing down the reasons why you're overweight and what you would like to do about it. Having this information down in a neat and tidy list will make the task easier.

Next, you need to write down a few simple steps to follow. For instance, you should be able to identify the most effective way to start a new exercise routine, whether you're a novice or a pro. However, if you do not have a realistic time frame, you might end up with a plan that is useless. Another useful plan is to use a peer support group. This can be something as simple as being able to check off your list, or as complex as receiving a new pair of shoes or a new book. Keeping a daily schedule helps you to stay on track. Also, having a visual cue like a calendar or a dashboard will show you what you have done and help you to focus on what you need to do.

As with anything in life, you will have to adapt to change. If you have to make a change in your lifestyle or you have a big life decision to make, you may need to change your mind or make a few adjustments to your current plan. But if you are able to keep your chin up, you should be able to overcome any challenges that come your way.

Chapter 2.
Retirement Pitfalls

Retiring without setting aside the first three years of income

When it comes to retirement planning, there are a variety of financial professionals who have come up with their own rules of thumb. While they're not always applicable, they do provide more insight than just "save as much as you can" and "be sure to save the best possible savings for retirement".

For example, some financial experts recommend saving three times your current income by the time you're forty. They also suggest saving a little bit more, such as twenty to thirty percent of your pre-tax income. Keeping a record of these contributions can help you see how much you've saved and keep you on track with your savings goals.

If you are lucky enough to have a retirement savings plan, you may be able to delay tax payments until you retire. Of course, you won't be making the contribution yourself, but it's still a great idea. You might also consider investing in real estate and blue chip stocks.

Another savvy way to start is to invest in a brokerage account, which can earn higher returns than a savings account. Investing in an alternative source of funds, such as short-term bond funds or money market accounts, can also be a safe and easy way to increase your savings.

Finally, you'll want to consider an emergency fund. A good rule of thumb is to set aside 3 to 9 months worth of expenses in case you lose your job or your home. Keep in mind that you can also supplement your retirement fund with a Roth IRA, which allows you to pay taxes up front.

Travel is a big part of retirement, and you should expect to spend a lot of it. Also, healthcare is likely to rise as you age, which means that your spending budget might need to adjust accordingly.

Remember that a radically reduced standard of living isn't a "golden age" dream. Be smart about your finances, and you can enjoy a successful, happy, and financially secure retirement. As a matter of fact, your retirement may be the best thing you've ever done!

Borrowing from your retirement fund

Borrowing from your retirement fund can be a very convenient source of quick cash, but there are many risks that are associated with this type of financial transaction. If you are thinking about borrowing from your 401(k) account, you should consult an independent financial advisor. Similar to a 401(k) plan, a 403(b) plan has a set annual contribution limit and allows for payroll deductions.

If you borrow from your retirement fund, the money you borrow will be taken out of the market and will not be earning dividends until it is repaid. Also, your investment returns will not be as high, meaning you will be missing out on a significant amount of earnings. Lastly, you may have to pay taxes on your loan.

Borrowing from your 401(k) is an option, but it should be used only in an emergency. This is because it is a form of debt and you could be mortgaging your future. While you will not have to pay income tax on the money, you will not have access to the money until you have repaid the loan.

The biggest risk is not being able to pay off the loan. In fact, you may have to borrow from your 401(k) again in the future. To be on the safe side, you should consider other options such as a no-interest credit card.

Getting a 401(k) loan is a relatively easy process. Depending on the plan, you can apply online, through the company's payroll department, or by contacting the plan administrator. For many people, a 401(k) loan can be the perfect solution to a short-term financial need. When you consider the benefits and risks, you can make a better decision.

Forgetting to account for health care costs

Many retirees forget to budget for health care costs when estimating expenses in retirement. But the costs of medical care are part of every budget. If you can't afford your bills, your health will suffer.

Health care costs accounted for 17.9 percent of the gross domestic product in 2010, but they are projected to rise to 20 percent by 2020. The cost of healthcare has a disproportionate impact on different groups of people.

Those with lower incomes and uninsured adults are more likely to suffer from high costs and lack access to care. This problem can lead to missed diagnoses, delayed care, and higher costs. There is also a need to address health inequities to ensure that all people can afford their bills and get the care they need.

People without health insurance often worry about their deductibles and premiums, and about unexpected medical bills. One third of adults say they have delayed recommended health care due to costs.

Healthcare costs can vary greatly from state to state, depending on your state of health and where you live. These sites allow you to browse providers and compare prices, and you can find discounts when you prepay online.

Similarly, if you have insurance, you can save a lot of money by using the Healthcare Bluebook. This site uses data from insurance claim databases to estimate the price of medical care. It also estimates administrative costs and billing costs.

Using these estimates, you can choose whether you want to pay in cash or with an insurer. If you do, you could be owing a bill that is more than you can afford, which can negatively affect your health and quality of life. For many, this debt is owed to credit cards, bank accounts, and other lenders.

Also, it can cause you to skip medications and other treatments. Some people are even unable to fill prescriptions because of high costs.

Ultimately, health inequities can have a profound impact on our health, our well-being, and the health of our system as a whole. These inequities also create avoidable costs and can result in major consequences for individuals and organizations.

When we think about the future, it is important to consider these issues so that we can mitigate the future consequences of inequity. As we continue to develop a health system that meets the needs of all people, we need to do more to combat health inequities.

Chapter 3.
Planning for Health Care Expenses

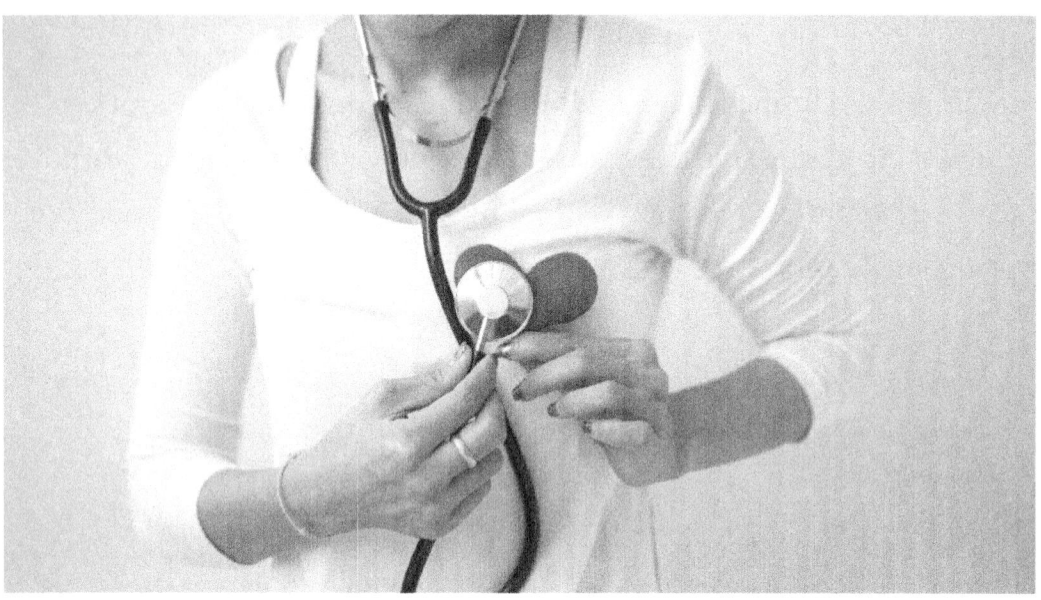

It's important to plan for health care expenses during retirement because they can be a significant part of your budget.

- Review your employer-sponsored benefits: If you are retiring from a job that offered health insurance, find out what your options are for continuing coverage.
- Consider setting aside money in a dedicated health care savings account to cover these costs.
- Eat a healthy diet, get regular exercise, and see your doctor for preventive care to catch any potential health issues early on.

Medicare supplemental insurance

Supplemental plans are available from different insurance companies. Depending on the company you purchase from, you may get a lower premium or more benefits than you expected.

As you get older, your premiums may increase more quickly than expected. In addition, the amount of your deductible and coinsurance may increase.

There are many different Medigap plans. Most of them offer the same benefits, but the plans do vary in price. Some plans may not cover some of the most common types of expenses, like long-term care and dental services. Alternatively, you can have an achieved-age-rated plan, which is based on your current age.

Disability insurance

It can be purchased through your employer or by an independent insurer. Most disability insurance policies pay out a percentage of your pre-disability income as a monthly benefit. In some cases, the insurance company will also pay for rehabilitation costs.

This can include modifications to your home, care expenses, and training. They may have a history of heart attacks or serious illnesses. Another reason for this may be that they are over 60. Often, these people have less income when they retire, and may not need to purchase disability insurance as much as younger adults.

However, if you do become disabled, you should contact your employer or the Social Security Administration to apply for disability benefits. A person is considered to be disabled if they are unable to work in a job they are trained for, or are physically unable to do their occupation. There are several types of disability that qualify, including total and partial disabilities.

Total disability is a type of disability that prevents the person from performing all duties in his or her own occupation. In some cases, this covers any occupation. For example, if an employee is a court reporter, and they have a severe orthopedic condition that limits their ability to write and speak, then their condition is disabling.

Long-term disability insurance coverage is a type of plan that provides a benefit for a longer period of time. This type of policy can pay for two, five, or even ten years. Benefits are paid on a monthly basis until you recover or the coverage expires.

You can add riders to your individual policy to cover your cost of living if you become disabled. These can be a good way to make sure that you are financially stable until your work is resumed. Having a source of income can be vital for people who are disabled.

Your insurer will consider your health and your occupation when assessing your risk for becoming disabled. A few common injuries and illness that can be covered by disability insurance include accidents, illnesses, and pregnancy. Also, if you have a family member who is disabled, you can apply for a compassionate disability benefit.

Health savings accounts (HSAs) and roth IRAs for health savings

Health Savings Accounts (HSAs) and Roth Individual Retirement Accounts (IRAs) are both types of financial accounts that can be used to save for healthcare expenses and retirement, respectively.

Both HSAs and Roth IRAs can be good options for saving for different financial goals, but they have different eligibility requirements and tax implications.

Health care options before age 65

Health care is one of the biggest expenses a retiree faces, especially in early retirement. Fortunately, there are many options available. A good place to start is with your employer's health plan.

You might be able to continue coverage with COBRA, or you can use Medicaid, short-term health insurance, or a healthshare. While this plan can provide you with health benefits, it doesn't cover any medical services outside of its territories. However, if you are in need of medical treatment, it can be very helpful.

If you are interested in this type of coverage, you should apply for it during the three months before your 65th birthday.

These plans usually don't offer comprehensive coverage, but they are cheaper than other types of health insurance. They are not regulated in the same way that traditional health insurance is, so you should be careful when selecting one.

Also, some plans may have high deductibles or caps, making them a poor choice for seniors who are active and have a need for frequent medical care. Another option is to apply for a HSA, or health savings account. HSAs are tax-free if you spend them on eligible medical expenses.

Some states also offer Medicaid for adults under age 65. In many cases, Medicaid can be the most affordable plan for low-income seniors.

The downside is that you must meet the income and coverage requirements, and your monthly income must not exceed a certain amount. Before you apply for Medicaid, you should check with your state to determine how the application process will work.

The ACA established a public health marketplace, called the Marketplace, where you can choose from a range of plans and find a health plan that fits your needs. Part-time jobs with health benefits are another option.

These are often less demanding than full-time jobs, but they can be a great opportunity to earn some extra money and learn new skills. Especially for married couples, a part-time job with health benefits can make it easier to stay employed until Medicare eligibility.

It is always a good idea to consult with an experienced health insurance agent when you are looking for a health plan, especially if you have a pre-existing condition. Most short-term plans are not designed for people with medical conditions.

Chapter 4.
What to Do If You Don't Have Enough Savings

- Setting up automatic bank transfers is a great way to save. Similarly, keeping all your money in one account will make the process easier. You should also keep a running spreadsheet of your progress.
- The most obvious reason to save is to have a rainy day fund. This can be used for unexpected bills or a dream vacation. If you do not have an emergency fund, you may need to use a credit card or resort to borrowing from the bank.
- Using the wrong savings strategy can actually be counterproductive. On the other hand, if you separate your money into different accounts, you can maximize your return on investment. Another reason to have multiple savings accounts is to reduce your dependency on interest-bearing loans.

- Many people fail to take advantage of their golden years, mainly because they haven't figured out a way to save for it. While it can be tempting to just buy a new couch or go on that fancy cruise you've always been eyeing, the wisest choice is to put that money towards a savings account. For example, if you're aiming to get out of debt, you should set a goal of paying off your most expensive debt first. Similarly, if you're trying to save for your dream home, you need to set a down payment goal.
- Finally, the biggest misstep when it comes to saving is ignoring your budget. However, just setting up a budget doesn't mean you're going to stick to it. Some common mistakes people make when it comes to figuring out their budget are to ignore their spending habits or to simply forget.

Working longer to boost savings

If you're looking to improve your retirement savings, working a little longer may be the way to go. While this won't necessarily mean that you'll have more money to spend, it could make a big difference over the long run.

The IRS recently announced new rules lowering the annual contributions allowed for IRAs and other tax-deferred retirement accounts. This might not sound like a big deal to some people, but it's actually a huge boon to those saving for their future. So even if you aren't in the market for a new job, putting extra money in a 401(k) or IRA can be a smart move.

In fact, you can boost your retirement income by working a few extra months per year. One example of this is the "4/10" program, which allows state employees to work four 10-hour days a week. A study of Utah workers who were a part of the program found that morale improved, and that an extra day off each week could be a good thing for both the employer and the employee.

Another popular policy is the five-day work week. Companies such as Basecamp and Uniqlo have tested the idea, and have reported positive effects. But while this type of schedule might be nice, there are also industries where a shorter workday isn't worth the hassle. For instance, physicians might want to keep their eyes on the prize and work a little harder. They might need to pick up more shifts or take on more calls.

There is no one-size-fits-all solution, so consider the specific circumstances in which you find yourself. If you are a higher-earning worker, you might benefit more from adding a few more days to your workweek, but if you are a lower-earning worker, you might be better off avoiding such an option. You can also opt for a part-time position or look for another job in a more affordable city.

As you look at the long-term strategy for increasing your savings, don't forget to keep an eye out for the next big windfall. Similarly, you should prioritize the highest interest debts first, since that will free up some money for your long-term investment goals.

In the end, the best way to increase your savings is to be more deliberate about your savings. That means setting aside more of your paycheck every month, using a tax-deferred retirement account, and directing bonuses to your savings plan. It also means taking care of your emergency fund and your high-interest credit card debt.

Generating income in retirement

One of the important parts of retirement planning is generating income in retirement. For example, your source of retirement income will depend on how you structure your life in retirement. You may decide to work part-time or even start your own business. However, you'll need to consider your goals and risk tolerance.

The best way to generate a good retirement income is to invest in a diversified portfolio of high-quality assets. Another great option is to invest in a fixed-income vehicle such as a CD. These are easy to buy and can provide an excellent base of retirement income.

Variable-source investments such as real estate can also be used to generate income in retirement. When investing in property, you can buy residential homes, apartments, or commercial properties. A key to success is to ensure you understand the taxes and maintenance costs of your investment and to understand what the market in your area is doing.

An annuity is another method of generating income in retirement. A deferred annuity is a type of insurance product that lets you lock in a higher value of income annually. With a deferred annuity, you can invest your funds in a variable annuity contract, an equity-indexed annuity, or an equity-indexed universal life annuity. There are various benefits to this investment, such as a tax-deferred payout.

While it can take a little time and effort to make this happen, it's a relatively easy way to generate a hefty chunk of cash each month. In addition, rents often rise over time. If you own a rental home, you can deduct mortgage interest and depreciation from your taxes.

The aforementioned 401(k) and Individual Retirement Accounts are great ways to generate a retirement income. As long as you don't spend all of your money on frivolous purchases, you should be able to retire with a healthy nest egg. Keeping some of these assets in fixed-income vehicles can mitigate the effects of inflation on your portfolio.

Other possible sources of income include dividend-producing investments, such as stocks. Dividends can be issued on an annual or monthly basis. They may be a good fit if you are looking for the most predictable form of income.

Finally, a bank account is a good place to put assets that you may need to spend on a short-term basis, such as an emergency. Banks typically offer competitive interest rates.

Creating a retirement plan

A retirement plan is a crucial step to prepare for your retirement. It ensures financial stability after your career is finished. It also enables you to safeguard your property and provide for your future.

Generally, you will need to start saving for your retirement well before you reach retirement age. As a rule of thumb, you will need to save more than you need to pay for everyday costs in order to fight the effects of inflation.

If you are married, you must factor in your partner's needs as well. Your spouse may be living a different lifestyle than you, and your plans for the future may be affected by theirs.

Another factor you should consider is health care. The cost of medical care is expected to rise. Make sure your plan includes health insurance and medical coverage. Also, you should take into account any complex medical conditions that you may develop during your retirement years.

When creating a retirement plan, it is also essential to calculate the amount of money you will need to live a comfortable, happy senior life. There are many factors you must take into account, including the amount of income you expect to receive, the cost of living, and other factors. Many people underestimate the expenses they will encounter during their retirement years. Investing your assets in a tax-advantaged account is an ideal way to generate an income for your retirement. Most employers allow direct deposits into a retirement account. Other sources of income include pensions, Social Security, and annuity payments.

Depending on your circumstances, you might choose to have an advisor work with you to help you meet your goals. They can also assist you with riding out volatile markets and managing your investments. Advisors can help you select products and customize a plan to fit your needs.

Chapter 5.
Housing Decisions

As people approach retirement, their housing decisions can be a significant factor in ensuring a comfortable and secure retirement. One important decision that retirees must make is whether to continue living in their current home or to downsize to a smaller, more manageable property.

Retirees may also consider the potential for rental income, the accessibility of the home, or the need for long-term care. A reverse mortgage can also be an option, it allows homeowners 62 or older to access the equity in their homes without selling or making monthly payments.

It is important for retirees to carefully weigh all of their options and consider factors such as cost, lifestyle preferences, and future needs before making a final decision about where to live in retirement. Consulting with financial advisor and estate attorney is also helpful to consider all the angles.

Another important factor to consider when making housing decisions in retirement is the cost and maintenance of the property. Retirees may want to consider a home that requires less maintenance and is more energy-efficient, to save money on utility and repair costs. Some retirees may also choose to explore other housing options, such as renting or shared housing arrangements, which can be a more affordable and less burdensome option.

It's also crucial to keep in mind the future needs, retirees may have to anticipate their long-term needs for assistance with daily activities and healthcare. A home with features like single-story living, wide doorways, and grab bars can make it easier for retirees to age in place. or considering a home in a community that offers services and programs that support older adults can help retirees plan for the future.

In summary, retirement housing decisions are a multifaceted and personal matter, and retirees should consider a range of factors including lifestyle, location, cost, and future needs before making a decision. Retirement is a big transition and the right decision can make a significant difference in the quality of life in the golden years.

Do Retirees Move?

It's a question of the ages - do retirees move? A survey by United Movers, an international relocation company, revealed an overall trend of retiring baby boomers leaving small and medium-sized towns and cities in favor of more centralized destinations. The study also identified the most common destinations for retirees, with Florida leading the way.

The state has many attributes that make it a prime retirement destination, including low taxes, a warm climate, a wealth of recreational activities, and a low cost of living.

In addition to the aforementioned amenities, it also has a variety of tax-friendly features, such as no state income or estate taxes, no inheritance taxes, and low public transportation fares. There are even discounts available to senior citizens and retirees!

Another reason why Florida is so popular is the weather, which offers year-round sunshine. In fact, the northern part of the state boasts a significantly warmer climate than other areas in its latitude.

During the winter, the temperature is around 55 degrees Fahrenheit, with little snowfall. On top of that, it's one of the few states in the country that doesn't impose snow tax or a ice tax.

The state has also been a popular vacation destination for decades, as well as a winter haven for snowbirds. However, it's not just the tourists who flock to Florida - it's also home to a slew of retirees looking to kick back and relax.

Whether you want to take a golfing lesson, go fishing, or simply enjoy a nice glass of wine on the beach, you'll find plenty to keep you busy.

Getting out and about is the best way to enjoy your golden years. Whether you prefer walking along a scenic river or taking a brisk bike ride, Florida has what you're looking for. Many retirees are selling their forever homes and moving into retirement communities, as the prices of real estate in their former stomping grounds are soaring.

Other reasons to consider the Sunshine State include low housing prices and tax breaks, a lack of state income or estate tax, and a wealth of outdoor activities. Retirees can also get a head start on their move by selling their current home or renting out the property.

Ultimately, it's important to determine the best place for you to call home when you reach the golden years. Consider the location based on your budget, health status, and family preferences before committing to a place.

Characteristics of a Good Place to Live in Retirement

If you are retiring, it is important to choose a good place to live. There are many factors to consider when choosing a location, including safety, health care, financial resources, and recreational opportunities. It is essential to use all your senses to evaluate a new location.

The first thing you should check is if a city is safe. You should always keep your family and friends close, but you should also consider the quality of health care available. A home with stairs is not an ideal choice for a retiree.

The cost of living can be an important factor when choosing a new city. It may be worth considering an affordable option. Some cities offer a good price-to-quality ratio, meaning you can enjoy the comforts of a retirement home while keeping costs under control.

Another consideration is crime rates. While you may not like to be in a high-crime area, you should still be aware of any potential risks. WalletHub ranked 180 cities on a number of criteria, including cost of living, crime, and accessibility to health care facilities. Using these factors, the company compiled a list of the best cities for retirees.

Panama, a small country located in Central America, offers warm tropical weather. It is tempered by the Pacific Ocean on one coast and the Caribbean Sea on another. Panama has modern infrastructure, excellent medical services, and friendly people. Despite its size, it is one of the three carbon-negative countries on Earth.

Many retirees prefer to live in locations that are convenient for friends and family. When moving to a new city, you should consider the social environment, and the costs of traveling.

However, it is also important to remember that you will not be able to spend as much time with your family and friends as you would at your own home. Besides, relocating to save money can be a jolting experience for older adults.

In addition, if you want to stay active in your retirement, you should consider a location that allows you to do so. Cities like Philadelphia offer a wide range of cultural and recreational options, allowing you to continue to live a fulfilling lifestyle.

For a more affordable option, you might consider Brownsville, Tennessee. This town features a vibrant downtown with numerous amenities, including restaurants, stores, and parks. Home prices can be less than the national median of $407,600, making it an attractive choice for retirees.

Other good choices include Danville, Illinois, and McAllen, Texas. These cities offer residents a reasonable price tag for a retirement home, while still providing excellent access to recreation and health care. Choosing a house that is not only easy to maintain but also safe to live in can make all the difference in the world.

Choosing the right house will help ensure that your transition into retirement is as comfortable as possible. Homes with extra rooms and windows allow for natural lighting, boosting your vitamin D intake.

Reverse Mortgages Are Not For Elderly Homeowners

Reverse mortgages are a type of loan that uses the equity in your home. These loans can be a great source of income for older homeowners. If you are looking for a way to tap into your investment, it is a good idea to consult a trusted financial professional. A CPA can help you evaluate your financial situation and determine whether or not this is the right choice for you. They will also be able to provide a number of possible payment options.

Reverse mortgages are often marketed to elderly homeowners. However, they can be beneficial for a variety of different situations. Those who want to access funds for medical expenses, retirement, or other purposes can benefit from the loan. Depending on the product, you can receive a lump sum or a series of monthly payments.

For instance, a married couple born in 1951 might decide to use the lump sum at closing to fund a college plan for their grandchild. However, if the couple dies, their heirs will have to repay the balance. The heirs can choose to sell the home or take out a traditional mortgage to pay off the loan.

Alternatively, the reverse mortgage can be used to cover the cost of a move to a new residence. However, you will have to stay current on property taxes, insurance, and homeowners association dues. Additionally, if you are moving to an assisted living facility or other housing that is not your primary residence, you will need to continue to make payments.

Choosing a reverse mortgage can be a great solution if you are in a difficult financial position and have little cash to spare. However, it can also be expensive, so it is important to be well informed about the process. Moreover, you can take advantage of the services of a counselor, a CPA, or a friend who is familiar with the financial aspects of this financial option.

Getting a reverse mortgage is not the first option you should consider when planning for your future. Instead, you should consider other types of financial products that offer a similar benefit.

For example, a Home Equity Conversion Mortgage (HECM) can be used to purchase a condominium or single-family home. This loan is backed by the Federal Housing Administration, which guarantees 95 percent of the appraised value.

Other types of reverse mortgages include those that allow the homeowner to receive a line of credit, a combination of payments, or unscheduled payments.

Deciding to Stay at Home Or Downsize

Deciding to stay at home or downsize can be a complicated and stressful process. When you downsize, you may have to get rid of your belongings or modify your home to make it more affordable. There are also costs involved, but downsizing can help you reduce stress, save money, and improve your quality of life.

Depending on your age and income, downsizing can mean different things for different people. Some seniors will downsize to a smaller space to help them live a more simplified lifestyle, while younger people may want to downsize in order to cut down on their housing costs.

This will allow you to know what furniture you'll need to throw away and what you can keep. You can then decide whether you want to move all of your items or just the ones you're not sure about.

In addition to determining the size of your new home, you'll also need to figure out how much you're going to pay to move. Having a moving company help you out can help you make the process easier, but the price can vary. It's best to calculate your moving expenses ahead of time, so you won't have any surprises.

Other costs associated with downsizing include selling your current home and moving to a new community. The cost of selling a home can depend on your neighborhood and the housing market in your area.

As you shop for a new home, you'll also need to consider your property tax rate. Moving to a lower tax rate can free up some of your budget, making it easier to meet your monthly bills.

No matter what your reasons for downsizing, it's always a good idea to talk with a real estate agent about the details. They can help you determine how much money you'll need to sell your home, if you're buying a new home, and if you'll need to make any changes.

Renting Vs. Buying a Home

If you have decided to buy a home, you are considering a large financial commitment. Buying a home involves many aspects, including short- and long-term costs, building equity, and ongoing maintenance.

In order to make the best decision, you need to weigh the pros and cons of both options and consider your own personal goals. Owning a home can be ideal for some people. For others, renting is more suitable. This is a benefit for young adults who are exploring career opportunities.

When the time comes to buy, they have time to save for a mortgage. Additionally, they can take their time to find a new house. The flexibility of renting allows them to test different living spaces and decide where they would like to settle. Renting may seem like the easier option, but it can be a big mistake.

You may end up paying more than you would have paid if you had bought a house. A rental can be more affordable, but you will not build home equity or have any tax benefits. Homeownership can be a great option for families with children. However, there are a few drawbacks.

If you need to relocate frequently, owning a home will be difficult. And if the housing market plummets, you could lose your investment. As a result, you should carefully monitor the housing prices in your area. Having a mortgage is a major commitment. Many people end up with underwater mortgages.

These homes can be a financial loser, but they can be a huge gain if the housing market improves. There are also taxes and maintenance costs that you have to pay. But the upsides of owning a home outweigh the negatives, and it's a wise choice.

You should make a list of your goals, including how much you can afford to spend and how long you plan to stay in one place. After you have weighed these factors, you can decide whether you should rent or buy a home.

While you are weighing the benefits and drawbacks of renting or owning a home, keep in mind that it can be a life-changing decision. Consider your finances, your goals, and your vision for the future. You can use a rental or buy calculator to find the best financial options for you. Purchasing a home can be a big commitment, and you need to consider your budget before you make a decision.

Renting can be less expensive than owning, but it does not offer the same tax and maintenance benefits. Keep in mind that you will be required to pay for your own insurance. Also, you can only renew your lease as often as you need to.

Chapter 6.
Physical and Mental Health in Retirement

Retirement can be a time of profound change, both physically and psychologically. While the majority of retirees have little trouble negotiating the transition, many experience significant challenges.

For example, some retirees find replacement activities elusive. They may also feel socially isolated and lonely, heightening their risk of premature mortality.

Physical activity is important for both health and well-being. The right exercise can improve cardiovascular health and reduce sedentary behaviour. Taking regular walks and participating in organised sports can also be beneficial.

However, there is a lack of evidence about the best way to increase physical activity after retirement. Whether or not this is a good idea depends on the individual and their preferences.

A number of studies have shown that depression is a major cause of premature death, and that individuals who suffer from depression are more likely to retire early. This may be because they have a difficult time adjusting to life after work.

It is also possible that older adults who do not suffer from depression are more likely to experience a positive transition from work to retirement. Therefore, it is a good idea for all adults, regardless of age, to have a plan in place for when and how they will transition to retirement.

The benefits of leaving a career to pursue a more leisurely lifestyle can be significant. Retirement can provide a much needed respite from the rigours of working life. Some retirees experience a loss of self-esteem and sense of self as they leave their work environment behind. Others may miss the companionship and challenge of working.

Research on the links between retirement and health is complex. Some studies have shown that retirement leads to an enhanced sense of well-being, while others indicate that it has a negative impact on mental and physical health. Other research has demonstrated that a negative change in life after retirement is associated with worse health and greater disability.

Studies have found that post-retirement social interactions are linked to better health, while a lack of such interactions can have negative consequences. For instance, loneliness has been shown to be a leading contributor to premature mortality. Furthermore, a positive transition to retirement may lead to stronger family roles and community involvement.

As more and more people are entering retirement, questions are raised about the health care that is available. For policy reasons, it is important to assess the relative benefits of retirement and health care.

Health care should be a part of any retirement plan. Keeping in mind that the elderly are at an increased risk of illness and disability, it is advisable to take steps to improve your own health. Keeping up with your regular medical check-ups is a good start. Identifying any existing medical conditions is also a must. If you are unsure, get a professional opinion.

It is hard to say how retirement will impact your health, but taking the time to learn about and engage in a wide range of options can make a difference. A healthy diet, regular medical checks, and regular physical activity are a few recommendations.

How the Body Changes After Age 65

Aging is a gradual process that involves a number of changes in the body. Aging can affect the skin, too. Kidneys also shrink with age. As the number of kidney cells decreases, they become less effective at removing waste products.

They may also excrete too much water. Other changes include a decrease in calcium and vitamin D. Having adequate levels of these nutrients is essential to preventing osteoporosis.

Older people also tend to suffer from chronic illnesses. Among the most common are heart disease, stroke, dementia, and diabetes. Taking care of yourself helps to keep your immune system strong and healthy. Another problem with aging is that the endocrine system, which regulates your emotions and body temperature, is affected. Many older people are active athletes, but even those who don't participate in sports can benefit from a healthy diet and moderate levels of exercise. Exercise can enhance the action of insulin, which can also prevent type 2 diabetes.

Those who live in areas of the world where it is cold all the time or where the sun is harsh are at greater risk of developing vitamin D deficiency. Getting plenty of sunshine and a healthy diet are two important ways to prevent this. You can also prevent or treat osteoporosis.

As you approach retirement age, it's important to know the signs of aging so you can adjust to your new body. Some of these changes are subtle, but others can be severe. Keeping your body healthy can help you enjoy the rest of your life.

How to Stay Active and Engaged As You Get Older

Getting outside and engaging in physical activities is one of the easiest ways to stay active and engaged. You can walk, jog, ride a bike, or play sports with friends or family. If you aren't as physically active as you used to be, you can still build strength and flexibility.

You can join a yoga class, or try a gentle brisk walk. These can be good for your cardiovascular system, which can help offset the effects of joint and bone degeneration. Another excellent way to engage in physical activity is to become a volunteer. There are many churches and virtual services that allow you to connect with people with similar interests. Your time spent with others will also strengthen your bonds.

Another popular activity to engage in is to read. Reading is a great way to expand your mind, learn new things, and keep your brain sane. Some other ideas to engage your mind are puzzles and board games. One of the most fun ways to engage in physical activity is to participate in a museum. Museum visits require you to walk from exhibit to exhibit, which will keep you active and alert.

Another way to be active is to listen to an audio book. This will make the time pass by more quickly, and it is a great way to stay entertained. Even if you can't get out of the house, you can use fitness apps to stay motivated.

For example, you can download a walking app and post progress as you go. Alternatively, you can use a video call to stay connected with a friend while walking.

Regardless of the type of physical activity you engage in, it is essential to be active in your later years. It will help you enjoy a happy and healthy life.

Chapter 7.
Non-Financial Aspects of Retirement

The non-financial aspects of retirement refer to the psychological, social, and emotional aspects of adjusting to retirement and the changes it brings.

For many people, retirement can mean a significant change in their daily routine and loss of structure, purpose, and social interaction. This can lead to feelings of isolation, depression, and a sense of identity loss. To address these concerns, retirees may seek to find new hobbies, volunteer opportunities, or ways to stay connected with friends and family.

Retirees may also have to adjust to changes in their roles and relationships with their family members and friends. They may find that they have more time to spend with their spouse, children, and grandchildren, but may also find that they are less involved in the day-to-day lives of their children and grandchildren.

Additionally, retirement can bring about changes in one's physical and mental health. Some retirees may find that they have more time to focus on their health, while others may experience a decline in their physical and mental well-being.

In summary, non-financial aspects of retirement relate to the psychological, social and emotional adjustments that one has to make during this time in life. Understanding these non-financial aspects and taking steps to address them can help retirees have a more successful and fulfilling retirement.

Approaching Retirement As a Single Person Or With a Partner?

Whether you are approaching retirement as a single person or with a partner, there are many things to consider. Retirement can be a time of great change and transition.

Creating a plan to ensure you have everything you need can help you feel prepared and more confident as you step into a new phase of life. Having an emergency fund can also help you maximize your payouts.

The most important thing to remember is that you aren't alone. In fact, more than a third of adults in the U.S. aged 50 and older are single. Singles have more options for saving for retirement. However, it is crucial to build a robust support system in case of a health crisis.

Having a clear, concise plan for your retirement is the best way to start. You can establish a routine that you and your partner can follow. For example, you can schedule regular date nights to keep your relationship fresh. Having a shared list of chores and responsibilities can also be a good idea. You can also hire someone to handle those duties for you.

One of the most exciting aspects of a new retirement is being able to focus on the things that you enjoy doing. It can be easy to fall into a monotony as you approach your golden years, and the ability to keep your priorities straight can help you stay motivated.

Developing a hobby together can be a great way to reconnect. Keeping a journal or diary can also be a useful way to keep track of your interests. By writing down your goals, you'll be able to stay on track.

Aside from making an inventory of your assets and establishing a budget, it's also important to keep in mind that you should have an emergency savings plan. These should cover three to six months of your living expenses. Investing in a roommate can provide additional income, and you may also want to rent out your basement.

Getting the right medical coverage is a big deal for retirees. Fortunately, Medicare and Social Security are designed to protect you in the event you develop an illness or injury.

While you are likely to have a larger support system than when you were working, you might need to enlist the services of a medical professional to manage your care. There are many other ways you can keep your loved ones healthy during your golden years.

Finding Your Purpose and Passions

In the 21st century, finding your purpose and passions can seem like a luxury. If you're always on the go, you might not have much time to ponder what you really want in life. However, it is essential to your happiness to know what you want. Find a way to schedule time to refocus and enjoy your passions.

Once you've identified your passions, you can focus on building a career around them. You might choose to work with a human trafficking cause, for instance, or help create an environment in schools that encourages learning.

Or you may find your purpose in helping other people feel beautiful. Whether your passion is about education, making a difference in your community, or simply helping people, you will likely be satisfied with your choice.

It's important to remember that your ability to enjoy the process of living a good life and making a positive impact in the world is connected to your passions. The more you consciously work toward your goals, the more you'll appreciate the good in the world. And when you are able to appreciate what you love about the things you do, your passions will naturally grow and you'll fill your life with joy.

One of the best ways to find your purpose is by taking a step back and letting your mind wander. Focus on the positive experiences you've had in your lifetime. Write down four things that have been meaningful to you. Take note of the patterns, themes, or even the words that come to your mind. Also, think about the times when you felt most satisfied. These moments of satisfaction will be the starting point for your passions.

Another helpful way to find your purpose is by taking a closer look at the people around you. You may find that you can help make a positive impact by donating money to nonprofits, volunteering, or by driving elderly neighbors to the grocery store.

Ultimately, your goal is to live your life in the most fulfilling way possible. Doing so will allow you to experience the life you were meant to have.

Social Interactions in Retirement

Social interactions play an important role in older adults' lives. Research has shown that older adults are psychologically healthier when they have a wide variety of social relationships. This includes friends, family, and colleagues. They are also more likely to avoid some diseases like osteoporosis and Alzheimer's, and they can keep their minds functioning longer.

Retirement can bring about major changes to an individual's social network. Before retirement, a person's network may have a higher percentage of inner circle ties. However, this number drops as the individual approaches retirement. Similarly, a person's outer circle ties may not be as numerous. In contrast, the number of ties in the middle circle may not change much during a retirement transition.

As people approach retirement, they reallocate their social network ties to family, friends, and colleagues. This decrease in close ties is less noticeable among cohabiting individuals. Although it is not yet clear why this occurs, a loss of a spouse, partner, or friend might be one reason. Alternatively, a lack of social ties can be a sign of isolation, a condition that is more likely to lead to mental health problems.

While many studies have looked at the role of social interactions in retirement, little has been found about the impact of retirement on a person's overall social network. The National Institute on Aging reports that social connections can help keep senior citizens healthy. A study conducted at the University of California San Francisco found that individuals who were lonely or lived alone were at risk for early death. Moreover, socially isolated seniors are more likely to be physically unwell, cognitively challenged, and have a lower quality of life.

A new study suggests that the most beneficial aspect of retirement is its ability to provide opportunities to invest in existing relationships. Specifically, the research investigated how changes in a person's social network may be associated with their overall well-being. It found that a person's emotional intensity is increased by the presence of strong surviving ties.

This effect was seen in both married and unmarried individuals. The number of surviving ties also had a positive effect on a person's sense of purpose. Interestingly, this effect was not as strong among cohabiting subjects, perhaps because they may be more focused on their family and the social aspects of retirement.

While it may be true that the effects of retirement may be noticeable only in the short-term, the changes may be more pronounced after a few years. Some of the surviving ties are of a greater degree of closeness, which may explain the increase in the emotional impact.

Nevertheless, more research is needed to understand how retirement affects a person's social network. For example, it is known that social interactions play a role in preventing dementia and reducing the risk of cardiovascular disease. Other studies have shown that the effects of social interactions on a person's overall well-being are more positive in those who have a wide variety of friends and family members.

Creating a Daily Routine and Maintaining Relationships

A daily routine is one of the many things that help us to connect with our loved ones. Routines are fun and they can give you a sense of security and well-being.

They can help you to avoid getting overwhelmed and they can improve your life overall.

The important part of a routine is sticking to it. It can help you get a good night's sleep, reduce stress and make it easier to get things done. Also, it can give you time to spend with your loved ones.

You may have heard about a morning routine and an evening routine, but what about other types of routines? Some people like routines, others don't. Depending on your needs and goals, you can create a routine that will benefit you and your family. However, establishing a new routine can be challenging. Here are some tips to make the process go as smoothly as possible.

The first thing you should do is to assess what you're really trying to accomplish.

Creating a daily routine is not as difficult as you might think. There are plenty of ways to change up your routine in small ways. Try swapping chores with your partner or making a family movie night or pizza date once a week. These small changes can add up to a better and happier family.

Creating a daily routine is a good way to improve your personal and professional life. However, it's important to remember that routines can be addictive. So if you start feeling bored, consider changing the routine or adding in a new activity. Doing something new can be a fun way to get back in the swing of things.

The best part of a routine is that it can be as simple as a coffee in the morning or a few hours of tech-free time with your spouse at the end of the day. Whether you decide to stick to a routine or not, it can be a great way to build your relationships.

Chapter 8.

Medicare and Health Insurance

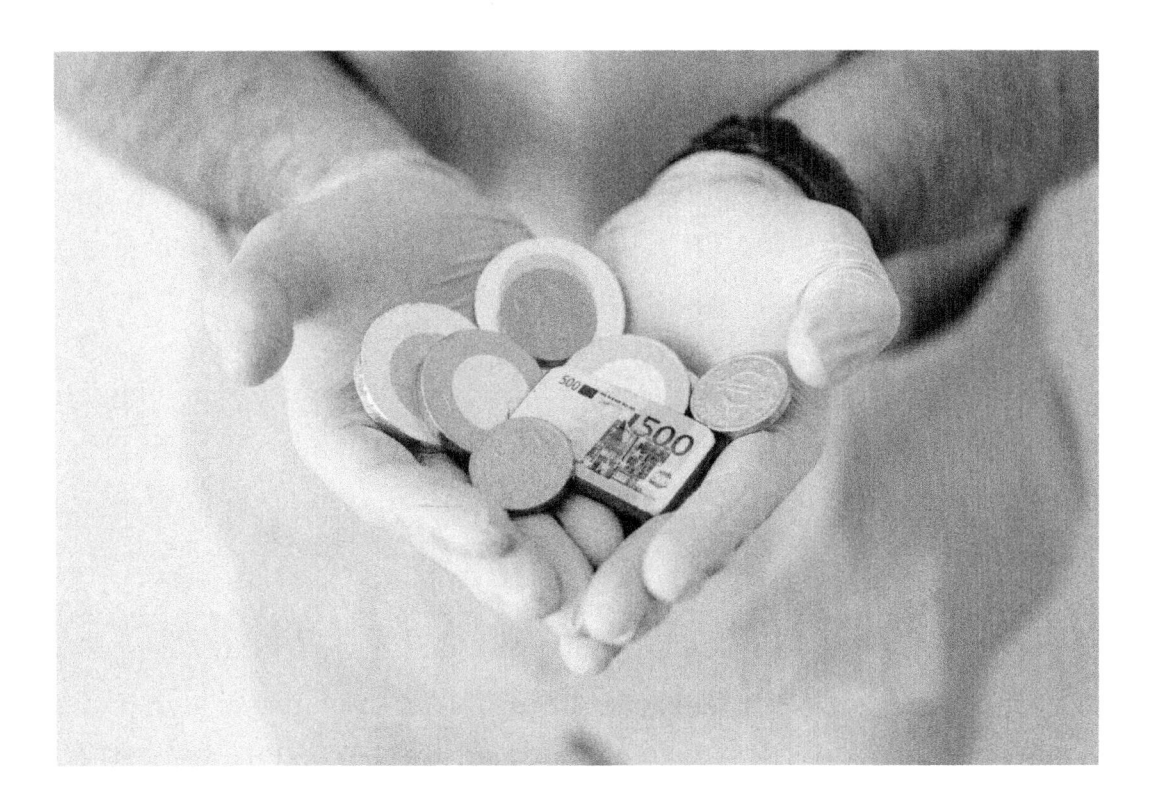

If you are not currently covered under an employer's group health plan, you will have to wait until the General Enrollment Period before you can sign up for Part A and Part B. When you do enroll in Part A, you can delay Part B for up to eight months.

However, you will need to pay a Part B premium for the rest of the year. For this reason, you should always compare the cost of your current employer's health plan to the cost of Medicare.

Many seniors rush to enroll in Medicare after they turn 65. While there are several options available, it is best to choose a plan after careful consideration. The

Medicare form is designed to be short and easy to understand. You will receive the form four to six weeks after you submit the necessary documents. Some forms are available in Spanish.

Another important thing to keep in mind when enrolling in Medicare is that Part D is available as a standalone plan. While it is not mandatory, it can be a good idea to have Part D. Part D covers prescription drugs. Depending on your income, you may have to pay more for Part D. In addition, the costs of Part D can change each year.

Finally, the Initial Enrollment Period starts three months before the individual turns 65 and ends three months after their 65th birthday. While this period is not mandatory, it is a good idea to sign up for it to ensure that you have coverage when you turn 65.

In some cases, people who are still working past the age of 65 can qualify for the Special Enrollment Period. If you are covered under an employer's group health plan and you have 20 employees or more, you are not required to enroll in Part B. As long as you are covered by the group health plan and you are not receiving any Social Security benefits, you will not be charged a late enrollment penalty.

Health insurance options before Medicare eligibility

If you're retiring before age 65, there are a number of health insurance options to choose from. These options will vary based on your income, healthcare needs, and lifestyle. But the Affordable Care Act (ACA) has made it easier for you to find and sign up for the right health coverage.

Before the ACA, people with pre-existing medical conditions had a difficult time finding and purchasing affordable coverage. For those with serious medical problems, it was impossible to get self-purchased coverage. However, if you were eligible for government subsidies, you could receive a tax credit to help with your monthly premium.

The ACA has created health insurance exchanges, or marketplaces, to provide an easier way for individuals to find and enroll in a plan. These marketplaces offer private health coverage for individuals and families.

There are also a variety of plans to choose from, such as short-term plans. Short-term insurance is a good option for those who need coverage for a short period of time. It can help you keep insurance coverage during a transitional period and fill in the gaps until Medicare eligibility begins.

Another option is to join a spouse's employer-sponsored health plan. However, some employers may not offer coverage beyond your retirement date. When you're signing up for your own health plan, you can talk to your spouse about the benefits offered by their company. Some people opt to take a part-time job with health benefits. While this can be a good choice for some, it's not as easy as it sounds.

You can also buy short-term health insurance on your own. These plans usually cost less than ACA premiums and can last anywhere from three months to a year. Although these plans don't cover any pre-existing conditions, they can provide coverage for unexpected medical expenses. Depending on your health, you may want to consider a longer-term plan.

You may also be able to stay on your employer-sponsored plan through COBRA. COBRA is a federal law that allows you to keep your group health plan when you leave your job. However, your plan may limit your benefits based on your age or medical history.

If you're retiring before age 65 and don't have access to employer-sponsored insurance, you can apply for Medicaid, a government program. This is available to people with low incomes. To qualify for free or low-cost coverage, you must meet certain income and asset requirements.

Another option is to sign up for Medicare, a government program that offers medical coverage for people age 65 and older. This coverage starts on the first of the month after you sign up. Typically, you will need to pay an annual deductible. If you don't have enough money, you can apply for Extra Help to cover the costs of Part D drug coverage.

Other health insurance options before Medicare eligibility include a Marketplace or short-term plan. Whether you need insurance for a few months or a few years, you can find the best coverage for you.

Understanding Medicare's ABCDs

If you are new to Medicare, you may not be familiar with the different parts of the program. But understanding the four basic parts will help you make the best choice for your health coverage.

The federal government provides health insurance for nearly all Americans over 65. Medicare covers many services, including doctor visits, medical equipment, and inpatient care. It also offers supplemental benefits, or Medigap, to help cover out-of-pocket expenses.

Part A is free to most Americans, while Part B pays for certain outpatient care and doctor office visits. Part D is designed to cover prescriptions. Most drugs are covered, but the cost can vary between plans. Some Medicare prescription plans require a monthly premium.

Medicare Part C, sometimes referred to as a "Medicare Advantage" plan, is an alternative way for Medicare to provide services. Many Advantage plans include Medicare Part D drug coverage. In addition, they may offer additional benefits like vision, dental, and hearing coverage. Choosing a Medicare Advantage plan is a good option if you are looking for comprehensive, value-based health coverage.

Original Medicare is the traditional fee-for-service plan offered by the federal government. It contains Parts A, B, and C. You can choose either of these options when you first enroll.

Depending on your state, you may be eligible to purchase a Supplemental Secondary Insurance Plan (SSIP). This is a private insurance policy that will cover some of the costs that Original Medicare does not. SSIP policies can vary in terms of benefits and costs, but they will typically offer the same benefits as Original Medicare.

Another way to get information about Medicare is to visit the website of the Kaiser Family Foundation. The site provides an overview of the program and a variety of resources to help you understand the details. Also, there is a free tool that can help you register.

Whether you are considering Original Medicare, a SSIP, or a Medicare Advantage plan, it is important to shop around to find the right fit for your health needs. When you enroll in Medicare, you are given the opportunity to choose your plan within seven months of becoming eligible. During this time, you may switch to a different plan if your current one does not meet your needs.

The Social Security Administration (SSA) administers the original Medicare program. Other insurance companies can sell you a supplemental plan. They may offer different benefits, but their policies will always be based on the same core values.

Getting more information about Medicare can be a daunting task. To make things simpler, the National Caregivers Library has a variety of free tools and resources. Besides the free tools, the library has a checklist that you can use to ensure you have all of the proper documentation for your Medicare needs.

If you need assistance with enrollment or are having problems with your Medicare plan, there are a number of trained volunteer advocates who can guide you through the process.

Using Medicare's research program

The Center for Medicare & Medicaid Services (CMS) awards grants for research projects to promote new health care financing and payment policies. These research programs involve all aspects of health care, including cost models, service delivery, and program design. By testing these policy proposals, CMS is able to identify important gaps in coverage and investment.

Using Medicare's research program to improve our health care system can help reduce costs and improve outcomes. This can result in savings for patients, more effective treatments, and improved health care for the country. Having a clear understanding of the costs of technologies and their benefits can also help CMS make more informed coverage decisions.

A key element of this program is the Merit-Based Incentive Payment System, which sets payment rates for clinicians who treat Medicare patients. In this program, clinicians earn points for meeting four performance categories. The MIPS includes bonus points if they meet specific conditions, such as electronic data sharing or interoperability.

Another key part of this program is the Medicare Evidence Development and Coverage Advisory Committee, or MEDCAC. It is made up of health care economists, medical ethicists, and public health experts. MEDCAC advises CMS on the use of evidence in its coverage decisions.

MEDCAC's expertise can help CMS make a more deliberate use of its coverage evaluation process. Instead of relying on time-intensive practice expense surveys, CMS should make more use of national coverage decisions. These decisions can be used to promote adoption of high-value technologies. However, the decision to allow or deny coverage is a separate decision from the decision to utilize a technology.

Similarly, the Center for Medicare and Medicaid Innovations can test and evaluate new approaches to health care delivery. While these projects are not required to meet federal standards, they do require a formal, transparent process.

Research funding is often granted by a specific CMS solicitation. However, unsolicited proposals are unlikely to be funded. If a researcher has an idea that might be of interest to CMS, they can contact the Office of Research Administration to find out more about their program. Alternatively, they can look at Fed Biz Opps announcements, which list grant opportunities.

The P01 program project responds to recent developments in the Medicare program and helps ensure that the program remains financially sound. Research conducted by the project encompasses a broad range of disciplines, from racial equity and prescription drug costs to the role of private plans in Medicare. There are three main areas of the research agenda: innovative analyses of current initiatives; future strategies; and the impact of current integration of financing and care.

Another key component of the P01 program project is the development of new guidelines for clinicians. For example, eligible clinicians will be required to show engagement with public health agencies.

Previously, these requirements were optional. Now, eligible clinicians will have to report this information to specific agencies within a specified timeframe. Providing this information can help increase clinician participation in the MIPS program, which is designed to promote health care delivery systems.

Annual open enrollment options and budgeting for health care expenses

During annual open enrollment, you have the opportunity to choose a new health insurance plan or switch one from your current plan. You can also add new benefits, like dental coverage, or enroll in a health savings account. The key is to find a plan that meets your needs and fits your budget.

For those who have health insurance through their employer, it is important to understand that your plan may change during open enrollment. Health care costs are projected to rise, and some companies are providing more options.

This can make the decision-making process more complex. If you have questions about your options, ask your human resources department or benefits representatives.

Choosing a health insurance plan during the open enrollment period is a great way to secure the best coverage possible. It's also a good time to look at your total health care expenses. That includes your premium, copayments, and deductible.

Considering a high deductible plan can help you save money in the long run. Many employers are now offering these types of plans to their employees. They typically cost more, but they offer lower out-of-pocket expenses. Depending on your needs, you may be able to save even more by choosing a plan with a lower deductible.

Other types of benefits include prescription drug coverage, vision plans, and dental plans. Some employers are offering virtual education to teach employees how to use these benefits.

While many organizations will start enrollment early, others will have a 30-90 day waiting period before benefits begin. When you choose your health insurance plan, you are choosing the option that will be the only one you will have until the following year. However, if you miss your annual open enrollment, you will have the chance to apply for a new plan at a later date.

If you don't have employer-provided insurance, you can still qualify for CHIP, Medicaid, or other programs. Those who qualify can apply for these programs any time of the year. Even if you don't qualify for any of these, you can apply for the Children's Health Insurance Program any time. To find the best plan for you, you will need to calculate your total costs.

Enter your household size, income, and ZIP code to get an estimate. Once you know your monthly premium, you can subtract your employer's contribution to an HSA, which will give you a good idea of what you can expect to spend each month. After you calculate your yearly costs, you can compare health insurance plans and find the best fit.

The next step is to decide whether to stick with your employer's plan or switch to a different plan. If your employer is limiting the number of plans you can choose from, you should consider a new plan. Otherwise, you might want to opt for a more affordable plan with more benefits.

Annual open enrollment can be stressful for employees. It can take weeks to research and select a new plan, so be sure to set aside time to do so.

Chapter 9.
How Retirement Has Changed and May Change in the Future

The public's attitudes and expectations about retirement have changed over the years, according to a new study by the Pew Research Center. While most people say they plan to work after retiring, a majority of those currently employed report that they plan to stop working at a later date than they originally planned. This means that retirement may be changing as rapidly as life itself.

In the 1990s, an Employee Benefit Research Institute (EBRI) survey reported that more than one-third of the workforce expected to retire before the age of 65. Today, seven-in-ten workers expect to continue working for pay after retiring.

Using data from EBRI's 2022 Retirement Confidence Survey, researchers found that nearly half of retirees will leave the workforce earlier than they expected to in that year. However, most of the changes are not driven by a lack of financial resources or poor planning. Instead, they are a result of shocks to the way people think about their retirement.

According to the Pew study, unretirement transitions are not driven by a lack of wealth or by a lack of good planning. They are a response to an unexpected health or financial issue. Unexpected issues can include layoffs, caregiving responsibilities, and other health-related challenges. These events can change where individuals live and their health, causing them to change their plans.

However, there are a handful of exceptions. Those who do not plan to retire at all are less likely to have an unretirement transition. These are called short unretirement spells, and they are excluded from the unretirement survival curve. Similarly, those who choose to call themselves retired are more likely to engage in behaviors associated with retirement.

Among the group that never worked, the likelihood of becoming unretirement was highest among the operators and laborers who didn't work, as well as the managerial and professional specialty occupations. It was also more common for the self-employed, college graduates, and those with a higher family income to expect to continue working after retirement.

Whether people plan to work or not is determined by the type of job they have. Among those who plan to work, the percentage of those who plan to work full-time is lower for those who are younger, have less education, and have a lower income. On the other hand, the percent of those who work part-time is higher for those who are older, have more education, and have a higher income.

Although there are a variety of reasons why people choose to retire before the age of 65, there are two main potential causes: economic and preference shocks. During periods of economic stress, people can be forced to work to make ends meet, or to meet their employer's needs.

When their health begins to fail, they may not have the resources to continue working, or they may not want to. Preference shocks occur when people don't like their retirement or don't have enough money to cover their expenses. Other causes of early retirement can be layoffs, health problems, and disability.

Future trends and potential changes in retirement planning

As people live longer and retirement planning evolves, it is important to understand future trends and potential changes in the retirement planning landscape. For example, there is an increasing focus on defined contribution plans, which have replaced pensions in most cases.

This shift has created a new competitive environment for firms to address in order to compete for market share and growth. While some firms have been forced to exit the market, others have been able to expand their benefits offerings to meet individual needs.

Another factor affecting the emerging trends in retirement planning is the rising cost of medical care. The NBER Retirement Research Center is working to understand how this trend is influencing the financial resources that older Americans have available for retirement.

The research also explores how benefit adequacy, payout streams, and financial market returns are influencing saving behaviors. In addition, the Center is exploring patterns of withdrawal from retirement saving plans.

Home equity has grown dramatically over the past twenty years. But recent turmoil in the housing market has raised questions about large changes in home values. However, the median savings account for adults in the U.S. is about $120,000, which is not enough to account for the rising costs of health care and other retirement-related expenses.

Many individuals have no idea about their options when it comes to retirement. However, there are ways to address this problem. For example, lower cost turnkey programs for small businesses can help unlock an additional $5 trillion in retirement assets. Having access to these programs can improve the level of retirement income that workers can access.

In the United States, the number of DB pension plans has fallen from nearly 175,000 in the mid-1980s to just over 47,000 today. DB plans were once the most popular option for saving for retirement.

With the decline in the number of DB plans, the retirement industry has been forced to shift away from traditional pensions and toward more flexible retirement solutions. These options allow workers to have greater control over how they invest their funds and when they withdraw them.

A recent ThinkAdvisor webinar explored the systemic change taking place in the retirement industry in the U.S. Panelists discussed how these changes are affecting the retirement industry and how to plan for retirement income. They also cited statistics regarding the optimal claiming strategies, illustrating the critical role that Social Security plays in retirement income planning.

There are also many other factors affecting the future of the retirement planning industry. One is the growing number of younger generations accelerating their retirement savings. Also, immigration has a significant impact on demographics.

People are living longer and retiring earlier. Moreover, many younger Americans are more concerned with short-term needs than long-term goals. So, as a result, it is necessary to plan for retirement in a more prudent manner.

Finally, an increased emphasis on personal responsibility for a better retirement outcome is essential. When retirement planning begins early, it is easier to achieve optimal results. It is also important to consider broader financial planning and investing.

Chapter 10.
Saving and Budgeting for the Coming Years

Saving and budgeting are important steps for achieving financial stability and reaching long-term financial goals. To save and budget effectively, it's important to have a clear understanding of your income, expenses, and financial goals.

To start saving, you should first determine a realistic savings goal and create a budget that allocates money towards that goal each month. Consider setting up automatic transfers from your checking account to a savings account to make saving easier.

When creating a budget, make sure to track all of your expenses and look for areas where you can cut back. This might include reducing discretionary spending on things like dining out, entertainment, or shopping.

It's also important to consider the long-term when budgeting and saving. This might include setting money aside for retirement, paying down debt, or saving for a big purchase like a home or car.

Overall, the key to saving and budgeting is to be consistent and to make it a habit. By regularly setting aside money and keeping a close eye on your spending, you can achieve your financial goals and secure your financial future.

Maximizing employer 401(k) contributions

Maximizing employer 401(k) contributions is a great way to save for retirement and take advantage of any employer matching contributions. Here are a few tips to help you maximize your contributions:

- Take advantage of employer matching: Many employers offer matching contributions on 401(k) contributions, so make sure to contribute enough to take full advantage of the match.
- Increase your contributions gradually: If you're not currently contributing the maximum allowed by your plan, consider increasing your contributions gradually over time to avoid a significant impact on your current budget.
- Take advantage of automatic escalation: Some 401(k) plans offer automatic escalation, which increases your contributions each year. This is a great way to gradually increase your contributions without having to think about it.
- Consider a catch-up contribution: If you're age 50 or older, you may be eligible for catch-up contributions, which allow you to contribute more to your 401(k) than the standard contribution limit.
- Take advantage of any employer's profit-sharing contributions.
- If your employer offers a Roth 401(k) option, consider contributing to that as well to diversify your tax liability.

- In summary, contributing to your 401(k) plan is an important step in saving for retirement, and maximizing your contributions can help you reach your goals even faster.

It's important to consult with a financial advisor and check your specific plan details to know the maximum contributions limit and the tax implications.

Reducing Expenses Is a Good Idea

Reducing expenses is a good idea, especially if you're looking to improve your finances. It can boost your net income and give you more capital to invest in other aspects of your business. There are several steps you can take to reduce expenses, from improving your marketing to reducing overhead.

The best way to find out how to cut expenses is to analyze your current spending patterns. Review your monthly and yearly expenses and compare them to your budget. You can also use computerized record keeping to spot inefficiencies. In addition, it is smart to look around for good bargains and negotiate better terms with suppliers. If you haven't checked out your bills lately, you may want to consider switching to a digital invoicing system.

A common cost reduction technique involves streamlining processes and eliminating redundancies. This will decrease the amount of time spent on manual tasks and free up that time for more productive activities. Also, automating tasks can be a good idea. For example, you might be paying for a project management tool with all of its paid features but don't actually use them. Similarly, you might not need to pay for a credit card processor if you have a better deal on the market.

Another way to save money is to buy in bulk. For instance, buying groceries for the month can reduce impulse purchases. Or, you can pay less for your cell phone if you can get a bundle. Make sure to review your bill every month and pay off any recurring subscriptions. Some subscriptions, like music, may not be necessary for your business.

One of the best ways to cut costs is to eliminate subscriptions. Whether it's for a teleconference service, a newsletter, or a magazine, cutting these expenses can be a big win for your bottom line. Additionally, you might want to consider offering discounts to customers who are already a part of your email list or mailing list.

When it comes to a purely financial exercise, reducing your expenses is the quickest and easiest way to increase your cash flow. It's also the most effective. Regardless of your business, you can benefit from lowering your operating and supply costs, which will improve your profitability and make your company more competitive.

By analyzing your company's expenses, you can start identifying and eliminating inefficiencies. For example, if you are purchasing new equipment, you may be able to recoup the cost by increasing your production. Likewise, if your company uses a shared supply chain, you might be missing out on great bargains. To help you find these cost savings, contact your usual vendors and shop around.

Other tips for reducing expenses include negotiating with suppliers and using technology to automate tasks. This includes using cloud-based services to lower infrastructure costs. Moreover, you might be able to improve your operational efficiency and reduce wait times by upgrading your equipment. Lastly, if you're a freelancer, you don't have to pay full-time wages and can instead opt for a subsidized rate.

Budgeting before retirement

Before you retire, it's important to have a solid financial plan in place. While you may have an idea of how much money you'll need to maintain your lifestyle, it's also important to know that your budget can change. By tracking your spending and keeping an eye on your accounts, you can make the right adjustments to keep your finances in shape.

To get the most out of your retirement savings, it's important to start thinking about your retirement budget well in advance. This can help you avoid making common mistakes and ensure that your money will last as long as possible.

The best way to figure out how much you'll need is to do a little research and get some tax advice. In addition to knowing how much you'll need to pay your bills, you'll also need to take into consideration the tax rates that you'll face when you retire.

While you're planning your retirement, you'll want to consider the aforementioned tax rates and the inflation rate. As a rule of thumb, you'll want to stick to a budget that allows you to enjoy a comfortable lifestyle for a long time. You can do this by comparing your income to your expenses.

If you have a low income, you'll need to save as much as you can, and you'll also want to cut down on expenses. There are many different ways to budget for a smooth retirement. Some of the more popular methods include setting up a budget, saving money, and using automatic savings to pay off debt.

Others use strategies like switching insurances and getting a roommate. However, the best approach is to work with a retirement expert, such as a Certified Financial Planner, to determine the best way to spend your money.

One of the most popular budgeting methods is the "needs-based approach." Typically, you'll have a fixed monthly cost for things such as housing, food, and transportation. However, you can't expect these costs to go down after you retire.

For example, you'll likely continue to spend on your car, and you'll have to make sure that your home repairs are taken care of. A good retirement budget should also include a fun budget. You'll have more time to travel, entertain friends, and indulge in other passions.

It's a good idea to make a list of these activities and include them in your monthly budget. Your budget will also include health care and other essentials, as well as some discretionary spending. Other things to consider in a retirement budget are: health insurance, investment portfolio performance, and inflation.

These are all things that you'll need to consider, so it's important to do your homework and keep up with the latest financial information. Additionally, you'll need to decide on a suitable retirement income, and you'll need to estimate how long you'll live.

Depending on your circumstances, it may be wise to wait until you reach the age of 70 to receive the full benefits of Social Security.

Conclusion

In conclusion, a guide to retirement is an essential tool for anyone planning to retire. It provides valuable information and resources to help individuals make informed decisions about their financial future.

It is important to start planning for retirement as early as possible and to regularly review and adjust your plan as your life changes. It's also important to seek professional advice when needed, such as financial planners or tax professionals. Remember that retirement planning is a lifelong process and it's never too early or too late to start. By following the guidance and advice provided in a retirement guide, you can increase your chances of achieving a comfortable and financially secure retirement.

It is also important to remember that retirement planning is not just about financial aspects, but also includes non-financial aspects such as planning for leisure activities, staying active and healthy, and maintaining social connections. A well-rounded retirement plan should take into account not just financial needs, but also how to make the most of your time and lifestyle in retirement.

In summary, a guide to retirement can help you create a comprehensive plan that addresses all aspects of your retirement, including finances, healthcare, leisure activities and social connections. The key is to start planning early, stay informed, and seek professional advice when needed. With proper planning, you can increase your chances of enjoying a comfortable and financially secure retirement.

Printed in Great Britain
by Amazon